O! Se ti jadinye nou ye.

Oh! We're little gardeners.

Written by
Mary M. William and Debra A. Harkins

Illustrated by
Macie Biesecker and Amber Rogers

Dedicated to

BPS children and their families

experiencing homelessness and poverty

Purple Owl Publishing
Newton, MA 02461
Copyright 2020
All rights reserved including right of reproduction
in whole or in part in any form
Follow us on Facebook @PurpleOwlPublishing

Magda ak Anna renmen ede timoun.

Magda and Anna love helping the children.

Yo deside anseye timoun yo kijan pou yo fè jaden epi plante manje kap kenbe yo an sante

They decided to teach the children how to garden and plant healthy foods.

toudabò, yo envite tout timoun yo pou aprann fè jaden epi manje pou rete an sante.

First they invited all the little children to learn about gardening and eating healthy.

Tout timoun tap ri epi jwe ansanm nan tè a pandan yap chache vè tè, goute tout kalite manje ak legim.

Everyone laughed and played together in the soil searching for worms, tasting different foods and vegetables.

Yo te li anpil liv sou fè jaden epi manje pou rete an sante.

They read lots of books about gardening and healthy eating.

Yo te fè dejnen ki gou ak legim yo te kiltive nan jaden an

The children made yummy lunches from the vegetables
they grew in the garden.

Magda ak anna te tèlman kontan yo te deside pou òganize yon gwo fèt kote yo te envite on pakèt moun epi te gen anpil manje ki te soti nan jaden timoun yo te ede kiltive.

Magda and Anna were so happy they decided to have a big party and they invited lots of people and had lots of food from the garden that the children helped to grow.

Le fèt la fini, Magda ak Anna te tris pou di tout bèl timoun entelijan sa yo orevwa.

At the end of the party Magda and Anna were sad to have to say goodbye to all the beautiful, smart children.

Pi ta, maladi COVID 19 la fè tout moun rete lakay yo

Then a bad sickness called COVID 19 made everyone stay in their homes.

Magda ak Anna te enkyete pou tout timoun yo ak fanmiy yo.

Magda and Anna were worried about all the children and their families.

Magda tap di: "Sa nou pral fè? Timoun yo pa ka jwenn manje epi you pa ka ale lekòl. Sa nou dwe fè?"

Magda said: "What are we going to do? The children can't get any food and they can't go to school. What should we do?"

Konsa, Magda ak Anna mete anpil manje ak liv nan sak epi pote yo lakay yo epi fanmiy yo te tèlman kontan.

So Magda and Anna made bags with lots of food and books and delivered them to their homes and the families were so happy.

Men te tèlman gen anpil timoun ak fanmiy ki te bezwen manje ak liv, plis manje ak liv pase sa Magda ak Anna te genyen.

But there were so many children and their families that needed food and books, more food and more books than Magda and Anna had.

On jou, pandan Magda ak Anna tap koupe dèyè zonyon yo pou mete nan konpòs, yonn te kontinye ap poze lòt kesyon, ki sa nou kapab fè pou ede lòt moun ki pa gen ase?

One day, as Magda and Anna were cutting the bottoms of the scallions to put in the compost, they continued to ask each other, what can we do to help others that don't have enough?

Yo tap reflechi, reflechi, reflechi.

They thought, and they thought, and they thought.

Anna di Magda: hmmm olye pou nou voye dèyè zonyon sa yo jete, mpral mete yo nan yon ti dlo pou m wè si yap pouse pou bay lòt zonyon.

Anna said to Magda: hmm, instead of throwing these scallion bottoms away, I'm going to put them in some water and try to grow new scallions

Magda di: Wi, m te fè sa deja, li te mache ak pòmdetè, fèy vèt, kalalou tou epi anpil lòt fwi ak legim.

Magda said: yes, I've done that before, and it works with potatoes and leafy greens and callaloo too and lots of other fruits and vegetables.

Bon se sa, se sa! Anna di, olye pou n kiltive manje pou nou bay fanmiy yo, nou te ka senpman ba yo plant ke nou fè pouse ak dechè ki soti nan legim yo.

That's it, that's it! Said Anna, instead of just growing and giving food to the families, we could just give families plants grown from these vegetable scraps.

Anna kontinye: nou ka mete yo nan ti po tou piti epi pote yo bay fanmiy yo pou yo kiltive manje yo yomenm.

Anna continued: We can put them in small pots and deliver them to the families and they grow the food themselves.

Magda ak Anna te renmen lide sa a tèlman ke yo te koupe dèyè zonyon yo, seleri, tèt kawòt, je patat ke yo te genyen epi yo mete yo nan ti goblè sou tèt tout fenèt yo.

Magda and Anna loves this idea so much that they cut all the scallion bottoms, celery bottoms, carrot tops, and potato eyes they had and put them in small cups all over their windowsills.

Apre kelke jou, zonyon yo te kòmanse leve, leve, leve.

A few days later, the scallion bottoms began to grow and grow and grow.

Se pa de kontan yo te kontan lè tèt kawòt yo te pouse fèy vèt epi seleri a te kòmanse jèmen.

They were so happy too when the carrot tops grew little green leaves and the celery began to sprout up.

Magda ak Anna te pran desizyon lè yo te wè jan zonyon yo te gwo pou yo te plante yo nan jaden yo.

Magda and Anna decided the scallions were getting so big that they should plant some of them in their garden.

Magda ak Anna te plante zonyon yo nan po tou piti, anmenm tan yo te prepare manje ak liv pou te voye bay tout fanmiy ki te plis nan bezwen.

Magda and Anna planted the scallions in small little pots and sent them along with food and books to all the families that had so much less.

. Fanmiy yo te trè kontan resevwa ti po yo pou kiltive pwòp plant yo.

The families were so happy to get the little pots to grow their own plants.

Pandan maladi COVID 19 tap kontinye, Magda ak Anna te fè videyo kote yap li liv sou jan pou fè jaden..

As the COVID 19 sickness continued, Magda and Anna made videos reading books about gardening.

Zanmi Magda ak Anna yo te tèlman eksite tou

Magda and Anna's friends were so excited too.

Tout moun te ede yo aprann ki jan pou yo plante dechè nan jaden yo.

Everyone helped them learn how to plant the scraps in their gardens.

Epi ki jan pou itilize legim ak fwi pou fè manje ki gou e ki kenbe moun an sante tankou pitza legim ak salad fwi.

and how to use their vegetables and fruits to make delicious healthy meals like vegetable pizza and fruit salad.

Epi tout timoun yo te aprann ki jan pou fè jaden epi pa gen pèsonn ki pat gen manje ankò.

And all the children learned how to garden and no one was without food again.

About the Authors

Mary M. William is a certified social worker, who recently retired from the Boston Public Schools (BPS) where she served as district liaison for 26 years. She founded Homeless Education Resource Network (HERN) that continues to operate by BPS. She is also the co-founder of *CEEDS4Change*, a non-profit organization founded in 2018. She previously served as a board member of the *Action for Boston Community Development* (ABCD) representing BPS. She is an alum of *LeadBoston*, a professional development program of the *Boston Center for Community and Justice* and is fluent in French-Creole as well as English. Mary lives between St. Lucia, West Indies and Randolph, Massachusetts.

Debra A. Harkins grew up in Boston, MA. For 25 years she's been teaching and practicing critical and community psychology. In 2007, she founded *Leading Change Associates*, a leadership development coaching and consulting firm specializing in diversity, leadership development, women's growth and non-profit human service organizations. She lives in Newton, MA with her husband and two mini goldendoodles.

CEEDS 4 Change

Acknowledgements

We have so many that deserve thanks for working with and helping *Ceeds4Change* to meet its mission of creating self-sustaining collaborations with public schools, higher education and businesses to reduce food insecurities in Boston's underserved communities by encouraging organic gardening, nutritious cooking and healthy eating. To *Ceeds4Change* board members Barthelemy Charles, Gwen Clark, Nneka Hall, Mariano Humphrey, Donna Lashus, Patrick Romain, and Renee Suchy for sharing a vision and mission to reduce food insecurities in the Boston area. Special thanks to C4C amazing Associate Executive Director, Amanda Ricko, for her passion and willingness to always step up for social justice—you are C4C future. To Judith Mathieu, Amelia Hall and Kerry-Pottinger for your gardening, cooking, and teaching that led to a highly successful summer gardening and cooking program for BPS students-in-need. To Sharon Holas and George Huggins, of *Ethnica*, for making nutritious food for C4C's COVID-19 response initiative. To McArthur Bertrand, MDL transportation, for transporting food to families-in-need during COVID-19 crisis. To *Mattahunt*, *Community Academy* and *Mildred Avenue* schools for working with us to meet the needs of Boston school children and their families-in-need. A big thank you to Nicole Doucette for her amazing teaching and cooking skills while making virtual cooking demonstrations for the C4C response initiative during this COVID-19 crisis. To Dr. Carmen Veloria who helped C4C obtain desperately needed funding that was used to purchase books for C4C COVID-19 response initiative and helped obtained financial support from *American Student Association*. To *Suffolk University* Community Psychology students who work with BPS students-in-need every semester. And special thanks to Boston Public school children and their families-in-need.

A huge thank you to Dr. Guy Apollon for translating this story into Haitian Creole and to our illustrators and beta readers.

Please visit us at:

CEEDS4Change Website
CEEDS4Change Facebook page
CEEDS4Change Instagram page

www.ingramcontent.com/pod-product-compliance
Lightning Source LLC
Chambersburg PA
CBHW041551040426
42447CB00002B/133